I. Introduction

Wealth is a key component of household well-being. A household's financial resources affect its ability to spend, to make long-term investments, and to weather shocks such as unemployment or illness. Household wealth often provides a more complete picture of a household's capacity along these dimensions than does income. As a result, understanding how households accumulate these resources is of central interest for policymakers and researchers.

Despite considerable research in this area, our understanding of household wealth accumulation in some ways remains incomplete. For example, some longstanding and more recent questions include:

- What are the major determinants of wealth accumulation? What are the roles of labor income, savings, capital gains, portfolio allocation, financial literacy, inheritances, and tax policy in wealth accumulation?

- Will households be prepared financially for retirement? Will defined-contribution pension plans prove sufficient as the main household tool for retirement savings?

- How do trends in income inequality, wealth inequality, and consumption inequality differ or mirror one another? How much mobility is there within the wealth distribution over short horizons as well as across generations, and what are the implications for the persistence of wealth inequality and equality of opportunity?

- How do fluctuations in stock or house prices affect a household's ability to fund an education, start a small business, or prepare for retirement? Is homeownership an effective wealth-building tool for lower-income households?

- What are the effects of student loans on a household's financial position in both the near term and long term? Does student debt, for example, impede some individuals' life outcomes and decisions, such as marriage, childbearing, homeownership, or career choice? Do student loans "pay off" over a longer horizon in the form of higher lifetime income and wealth?

1

- What is the relationship between debt and consumption? To what extent did "debt overhang" exacerbate the 2007–09 recession, and to what extent did tight credit conditions hinder the subsequent recovery?

- How will the Affordable Care Act affect household wealth accumulation? Will saving decrease because households have less of a need to self-insure against medical expenses? Will household wealth become less volatile, and will rates of bankruptcy or foreclosure filings decrease?

Because financial resources are accrued over a lifetime, data that follow households over time— that is, panel or longitudinal data—have the potential to improve significantly our understanding of the wealth-accumulation process and its determinants. The United States currently has three long-running panel surveys that include information on households' wealth holdings. The Panel Study of Income Dynamics (PSID) has collected wealth data since 1984 on a nationally representative sample of families; the 1979 National Longitudinal Survey of Youth (NLSY) has collected wealth data since 1985 on a cohort of individuals born between 1957 and 1964; and the Health and Retirement Study (HRS) has collected wealth data since 1992 on cohorts of households ages 50 or older.

Other surveys track changes in household wealth over shorter periods of time. The Consumer Expenditure Survey (CE) interviews households for one year, and, in the last interview, asks households about the current value of their financial assets as well as the change in the value of these assets over the past year. The CE, however, does not collect data on the value of some nonfinancial assets, such as businesses. The redesigned 2014 Survey of Income and Program Participation (SIPP) will collect wealth data over a three-year period. (Earlier SIPP panels collected wealth data for periods of differing length.) Finally, although the Survey of Consumer Finances (SCF) is generally a cross-sectional survey, the Federal Reserve has twice sponsored collection of panel data: households in the 1983 SCF cross-section were re-interviewed in 1986 and 1989, and households in the 2007 SCF cross-section were re-interviewed in 2009.

In principle, researchers should be able to address many of the most pressing questions about household wealth accumulation with these existing data sets. And in fact, the PSID wealth data have been used by Hurst, Luoh, and Stafford (1998) to explore wealth dynamics in the 1980s and

1990s; by Charles and Hurst (2003) to explore the correlation of wealth across generations; by Cooper (2013) to study the relationship between housing wealth and consumption; and by Dynan (2012) to consider the role that debt overhang plays in consumption. Numerous studies have used the HRS data to explore wealth changes before and after retirement—Love, Palumbo, and Smith (2009) and Poterba, Venti, and Wise (2011) are two such examples—as well as other aspects of wealth accumulation, such as family investments in college education (Brown, Scholz, and Seshadri, 2012). Zagorsky (1999) used the NLSY data to examine the wealth accumulation patterns of baby boomers in their first two decades as adults, and Bricker et al. (2011) explore changes in household wealth during the 2007–09 recession with the 2007–09 SCF panel.

In practice, however, measurement error and other data quality issues appear to constrain the usefulness of these data for research, particularly research focused on changes in the value of assets and liabilities over time. For example, Zagorsky (1999) notes, "Findings suggest that not cleaning NLSY79 wealth data causes non-sensical results." Bosworth and Smart (2009) indicate "the estimates of saving and the change in net worth for both the PSID and the HRS are quite volatile across subperiods and subgroups… the calculations are also affected by outliers in the reported values of the wealth components and active savings. Various algorithms for identifying those outliers indicate a substantial number of implausible answers to the wealth and saving questions, either due to problems in the original responses or coding errors." Similarly, Venti (2011) notes, "Troublesome outliers [in the HRS] are still plentiful enough to confound some analyses."

Does the United States need a new panel study on household wealth?

Our assessment is that these existing panel data sets may be insufficient to examine the determinants of household wealth accumulation for three reasons. First, many of these data sets are limited in their scope. The HRS and the NLSY collect wealth information for specific subsets of the population. The CE, SIPP, and 2007–09 SCF panels collect wealth data for short periods of time. Only the PSID measures wealth accumulation patterns for all types of households over an extended period. Second, data quality concerns make it difficult to draw clear or possibly even reliable conclusions about wealth and savings from many of these surveys.

Third, even absent measurement error, there is wide dispersion in wealth, and the samples sizes of existing panel data sets may be insufficient to yield precise estimates.[1]

Given the challenges of collecting wealth data, however, we think it would be unwise to create a new panel survey that includes wealth data without an accompanying commitment to: i) setting up data collection systems in which measurement error is less likely to occur (for example, by extensively pretesting questions and training interviewers); ii) comprehensive editing and imputation once the data are collected; and iii) consideration of whether the sample size is adequate. The noise in the existing data sets appears to have limited its usefulness for research, so there is little to be gained by creating new data that exhibit the same shortcomings. If resources are not available for addressing the measurement issues, we suggest collecting a more limited set of covariates that could serve primarily as useful controls for financial resources in analyses focused on topics other than wealth.

In the sections that follow, we explore some of the difficulties in accurately measuring wealth, gauge which wealth components appear to be relatively well-reported on surveys, and assess the implications of these findings for panel wealth data.

II.   Why are wealth data so noisy?

Accurate data on household wealth are notoriously hard to collect for several reasons, including:

- Households may monitor the values of their assets or the amount of their liabilities only sporadically, so respondents may be unable to provide exact values accurately without consulting documents. In addition, households may round their asset and debt values when they report them.

- The values of assets that are thinly traded or idiosyncratic are hard to measure. For example, although a homeowner may be able to gauge the value of her house from its tax assessment, web sites such as Zillow, or sales prices of nearby properties, these estimates can vary significantly from each other. These values generally will also not reflect

---

[1] Venti and Wise (1998), for example, document the wide dispersion in wealth among respondents to the Health and Retirement Survey, even conditioning on lifetime earnings.

differences across seemingly similar homes due to unmeasured, idiosyncratic features, such as upgrades, damage, or renovation. These values may also diverge from the homeowner's personal valuation (that is, the amount the homeowner would accept if she had no reason to move), and a homeowner will only observe the market value of her house at the time of its purchase or sale. Similarly, the market value of a small business may only be known upon purchase or sale.

- Even when the value of an asset or debt can be readily measured, a question may be phrased in a way that respondents find difficult to understand, or a respondent may not have the financial acumen to answer the question correctly. For example, Bucks and Pence (2008) demonstrate that the share of borrowers in the 2001 SCF that reported having private mortgage insurance (PMI) and the share that reported that the mortgage was federally guaranteed were both greater than the corresponding shares in lender-reported data. These discrepancies may reflect confusion of PMI with other types of insurance on the home and borrower misunderstanding of the phrase "federally guaranteed" (particularly the role of government-sponsored enterprises).[2]

- Money is an especially private topic, and households may be reluctant to reveal details of their personal finances. Some households may be more comfortable providing a broad range rather than the exact value of an asset. Other emotions associated with money, such as shame or embarrassment, may also lead households to provide inaccurate responses about the amount or even existence of categories of income, assets, or debt (see, for example, Tourangeau et al., 2000).

- The wealth distribution is skewed, and getting an accurate estimate of the full distribution or aggregate amount of wealth requires a concerted effort to identify and over-sample households that are more likely to be wealthy. Such households may be more difficult to reach, and less forthcoming with their financial information. The response rate in the broad-based random-sample component of the 2004 SCF (the area-probability sample),

---

[2] In line with this conjecture, the SCF added an instruction to interviewers for the 2007 SCF that Fannie Mae and Freddie Mac should not be included as federal guarantors.

for example, was 69 percent, compared with about 10 percent for SCF households in the portion of the list sample that is predicted to be most wealthy (Kennickell, 2006).

The challenges of collecting and disseminating reliable wealth data are even more profound for panel data than for cross-sectional data. For example, given the issues with collecting wealth data, any measured change in wealth—especially over a short period of time—may reflect measurement error as much as an actual change in household portfolios. At the same time, a household's financial situation can change dramatically over short periods of time for legitimate reasons. Individuals may, for example, inherit significant amounts of money, sell a small business, or incur a devastating expense. Therefore, researchers cannot assume that a large reported change is necessarily incorrect, and disentangling legitimate jumps in wealth from those induced by measurement error can be challenging. Major financial shocks to the household can further complicate measurement of household wealth over time if such shocks are correlated with the ability to follow households and to retain their cooperation.

An additional complication stems from the fact that wealth is typically measured at the household level, yet a "household" is not a stable concept over time. Household wealth may shift dramatically as individuals marry or divorce or as other people move into or out of the household. Although researchers typically use equivalence scales to adjust for such compositional changes in studies of income and consumption, no consensus exists on comparable scales for household wealth (OECD, 2013, Section 7.3.6). As the length of the panel increases, so does the probability of changes in household composition that may significantly affect household wealth.

Because wealth data are subject to comparatively high rates of missing or seemingly erroneous values, the data are often adjusted with imputation routines. The availability of data from earlier waves can be useful for imputing missing data in a longitudinal survey, but in general imputation is more complex for longitudinal data than for cross-sectional data. Finally, because of their sensitivity, financial and wealth data require close disclosure review and procedures to minimize disclosure risk, including potentially restricting data access. These concerns and the necessary steps to mitigate disclosure risk are heightened for longitudinal data because more information is available for each individual.

Measurement issues are a consideration even in the Survey of Consumer Finances, which is viewed as the highest-quality wealth data for the United States. Part of the reason for the SCF's success is that wealth data are the primary focus of the survey, and it has developed many procedures to increase the quality of these data, such as providing interviewers with specialized training on the components of household wealth as well as designing data-quality checks and imputation procedures tailored to wealth data. The accuracy of wealth data may be lower in surveys focused on topics other than wealth. For example, Zagorsky (1999) notes about the 1979 NLSY, "The wealth module is intentionally placed at the survey's end, to ensure that all other information is captured even if wealth questions offend the respondent and result in a refusal to continue. After answering questions for an hour, it is highly probable that respondents are tired and not answering as precisely as earlier."[3]

Even with this emphasis on collecting wealth data, the SCF data requires considerable editing. In the 2007–09 panel, for example, 40 percent of cases required "substantial" edits. These edits resulted in non-negligible changes to the wealth distribution—most percentiles of the edited wealth distribution differed from the corresponding percentiles of the unedited distribution by five to ten percent (Kennickell, 2014).

Hill (2004) similarly illustrates the importance of editing and review of wealth data in the Health and Retirement Study. Thirteen percent of households who answered the 1998 and 2000 HRS surveys and met other criteria also reported changes over that period of at least $50,000 in one component of net worth, and at least $150,000 in total net worth. These households were contacted to verify their data, and in more than half of the cases, the households indicated that one or more of the data pieces used to construct the change was incorrect. This finding suggests both a high rate of measurement error and the difficulty of distinguishing measurement error from actual changes. Correcting these issues reduced the variance of the measured change for the sample in half and improved the measured correlation of changes in net worth and income.

III.   What components of wealth data appear to be reported accurately?

_____

[3] In the subsequent 1997 NLSY panel, questions about drug-dealing and sexual activity are asked after the wealth module. This ordering aligns with the ranking of relative topic sensitivity from Bradburn, Sudman, and Associates (1979) as reproduced in Tourangeau et al. (2000).

Aside from data-entry and similar errors, measurement error in self-reported wealth data might be classified into two broad types: (1) the asset or liability has an exact value, but the household either does not know the value (possibly due to misunderstanding the question) or prefers not to reveal it (including possibly intentionally misreporting); and (2) the exact value of the asset or liability is not knowable or potentially ambiguous, as in the case of a small business. The first type of error can perhaps be mitigated through, for instance, refinement of survey questions or incentives for households to consult financial records; the second may be more difficult.

Researchers have taken a few different approaches to infer the potential extent of measurement error in survey data. One indicator of measurement error is the share of households who report that they do not know the value of an asset or a liability, or the share who report a range instead of an exact value. However, reporting an exact value does not rule out measurement error, as households may report a value that is incorrect. To explore this possibility, researchers typically compare survey data with administrative records. In the best cases, researchers can match these data sources for the same person and same account; generally, though, researchers are only able to compare aggregates or distributions. Finally, researchers with panel data can explore the share of changes in ownership or values that seem implausible.

Ownership of assets and liabilities

In general, households rarely report that they "don't know" whether they own a particular type of asset or owe a certain type of liability. Kennickell (2011) notes that, for the SCF, "variables indicating ownership or receipt of a given item… are rarely missing," and Zagorsky (1999) indicates "Very few individuals [on the 1979 NLSY] have missing answers for questions which determine whether the respondent has a given asset or liability."

To demonstrate this point more fully, Table 1 shows the distribution of the internal edit codes for the 2009 wave of the 2007–09 SCF panel for each of the ownership variables.[4] The edit codes show whether:

---

[4] All estimates in this paper, unless otherwise noted, were calculated using Stata 12.1 on a 32-core Dell server with 196 GB of memory running Redhat Linux. The 2007-09 Panel Survey of Consumer Finances data are available at http://www.federalreserve.gov/econresdata/scf/scf_2009psurvey.htm.

- the SCF staff deemed the response to the question as reasonable ("Original value");

- the initial response was edited, for example, if a respondent's reported defined-benefit pension plan looked more likely to be a 401(k) plan ("Edited value");

- the respondent reported "Don't know" or refused to answer the question ("Refused"); or

- the SCF staff set the value to "missing to be imputed" because the likely value (or, for dollar amounts, a range) could not be inferred ("Missing").

We consider any code other than "original value" as an indication that the household had difficulty with the question or that measurement error may be a factor.

For most categories of ownership of financial assets, nonfinancial assets, and liabilities, the respondent's original answer is nearly always used in the survey data. In contrast, a significant share of the responses are edited for retirement plans, the cash value of whole life insurance, and mortgages on properties other than the primary residence. In the case of retirement plans, the large number of edited values stems from respondents who reported different pension types in 2007 and 2009 for what was presumably the same plan, and from respondents who reported retirement plans in 2009 that appear to have existed in 2007, but were not reported then (Kennickell, 2011). "Edited" values are also a touch elevated for IRAs and real estate.

Because of the SCF question structure, the edit codes for the pension questions combine the responses to two questions: i) whether the respondent has a pension; and ii) whether the pension is an account type. The share of responses that were edited is somewhat lower for the "has a pension" question than the "type of pension" question (7 and 11 percent, respectively, for current-job pensions).[5] The difference is starker for cash-value life insurance, for which respondents are first asked whether they have life insurance, and then whether the policy could accrue a cash value. Less than 1 percent of the responses to the "has life insurance" question were edited, compared with 24 percent of responses to the "accrue cash value" question.

---

[5] The edit-code analysis for the "type of pension" question is restricted to respondents with a valid answer to the "have a pension" question. Likewise, the edit-code analysis for the "accrue cash value" life insurance question is restricted to respondents with a valid answer to the "have life insurance" question.

Other studies have also documented apparent inaccuracies in self-reported pension and IRA ownership. As suggested above, respondents generally know whether they have a pension but have difficulty identifying whether their pensions are defined-benefit or defined-contribution plans. Gustman, Steinmeier, and Tabatabai (2007) compare worker and employer assessments in the HRS of whether the worker has a defined-benefit or defined-contribution plan and find that these two reports differ more than one-third of the time. Many HRS respondents also report patterns of pension and IRA ownership over time that appear to be inconsistent. Venti (2011), for example, finds that about a quarter of HRS respondents report unlikely gaps in their IRA ownership, most notably indicating owning an IRA at some point in the 1992 through 2006 waves; subsequently reporting no IRA; and then reporting an IRA again in a later wave. Further, Venti finds that about 20 to 30 percent of HRS respondents who report that their jobs and pensions have not changed between two waves of the survey also report different pension plan types in the two waves.

As suggested earlier, ownership of other types of assets, including automobiles and homes, is generally considered to be well-measured. Koijen, Van Nieuwerburgh, and Vestman (forthcoming), however, offer a sobering exception to this conclusion. They match administrative and household-reported data on auto purchases in Sweden and find that households failed to report almost 30 percent of car purchases observed in the administrative data. Some of this discrepancy may stem from households misreporting when they purchased a car, rather than misreporting the purchase itself, or it may reflect shortcomings with the underlying surveys.[6] We tend to put less weight on this finding because it differs so dramatically from the negligible fractions of edited or imputed values for vehicle ownership in the SCF.

Values of assets and liabilities

Households appear to have more difficulty reporting the values of their assets and liabilities than in reporting whether they own the assets or owe the liabilities. In part, this pattern is by construction: the set of households who do not know the value of an asset includes both

---

[6] The Swedish household survey asks households whether they purchased vehicles within a certain look-back period.

households who do not know if they own that asset as well as households who know they own it but are uncertain of its value.

Table 2 repeats the earlier edit-code analysis for the variables corresponding to the asset and liability values. This table includes an additional category—"range"—for cases in which the respondents reported a range instead of an exact value, or in which the SCF staff re-coded a reported value as a range. The values in this table are calculated for households for whom the corresponding ownership variable was an "original value." We do so because, as noted above, other edit codes for the ownership values generally lead mechanically to missing values for the corresponding amount of holdings, and we want to isolate the extent of confusion, uncertainty, or reluctance specific to the value of a given asset or debt.

Financial assets, as ranked by household knowledge of their values, appear to fall in three broad categories. In the first category, around 85 percent of respondents provided exact values for transaction accounts, certificates of deposit, or savings bonds, about 10 percent provided or were assigned a range for these values, and less than 2 percent reported "don't know." In the second category, 75 to 80 percent of respondents provided exact values for bonds, stocks, mutual funds, IRAs, and Keoghs, around 15 percent of values were ranges, and 2 to 5 percent reported "don't know." In the third category, 60 to 70 percent provided an exact value for pensions from their current or past jobs, the cash value of life insurance, or trusts and annuities, around 15 percent were ranges, and 6 to 16 percent reported "don't know." The shares of "refused" and missing responses are quite small in almost all categories.

Nonfinancial assets also can be classified into three broad categories based on these reporting rates. First, nearly 90 percent of respondents provided an exact value for their home or automobile, 10 percent provided or were assigned ranges, and only a handful reported "don't know." Second, around 80 percent of respondents provided values for second homes, other residential real estate, nonresidential real estate, and actively managed businesses; 11 to 14 percent of values were ranges; and "don't know" rates were quite low, although a touch higher for non-residential real estate. Third, only 67 percent of households provided an exact value for businesses that they did not actively manage, with 17 percent being a range and 13 percent reporting "don't know." Refusals and missing values were low for these assets as well.

11

Household debt is generally well-reported, with 80 to 90 percent of respondents providing an exact value. Edited values and ranges accounted for the majority of other responses. Data quality is a bit worse for mortgages, as edited values, ranges, and missing values were a bit more prevalent for mortgages against the primary residence than for the other types of liabilities, and the share of respondents with non-residential real estate who responded "don't know" to its value is greater than the corresponding rates for other liabilities.

The patterns of "don't know" rates in other surveys are broadly consistent with the SCF. In the 1985 to 1996 waves of the NLSY79 data, "don't know" rates are 3 percent or lower for homes, mortgages, cash saving, cars, and household debt; around 7 percent for businesses; and 10 percent or higher for certificates of deposit, IRAs, 401(k)s, stocks, bonds, and trusts (Zagorsky, 1999). The codebook for the 2011 wave of the PSID also suggests that "don't know" rates are lower for transaction accounts, certificates of deposit, government bonds, houses, cars, mortgages, and consumer debt than for stocks, mutual funds, IRAs, 401(k)s, businesses, and the cash value of whole life insurance.

As a complement to this analysis, we review the fairly small number of studies that have gauged the quality of survey-reported data by comparing distributions and aggregates from those data to those estimated from administrative data. In the case of owner-occupied housing, some studies find that, on the whole, homeowners report their house values fairly accurately, whereas others find that homeowners tend to overstate their home values by five to ten percent.[7]

Estimates of aggregate debt derived from survey data and administrative data appear to be largely consistent for most types of household debts. Brown et al (2013) show that aggregate measures of mortgage debt, home equity lines of credit, and auto loans estimated from credit bureau files line up well with the corresponding SCF aggregates. In contrast, they find that credit bureau measures for aggregate credit-card debt and student loans are larger than the SCF measures, which may indicate that households under-report the value of these debts on surveys. Henriques and Hsu (2014), however, find that the distribution of credit-card debt, conditional on having such debt, is similar in the SCF and credit-bureau data, a finding that suggests that factors

---

[7] Some representative papers in this literature are Bucks and Pence (2006), Goodman and Ittner (1992), Henriques (2013), Kiel and Zabel (1999), and van der Cruijsen, Jansen, and van Rooij (2014).

other than household misreporting may play a role in the discrepancy in the aggregate measures. Henriques and Hsu also note that aggregate mortgage debt in the SCF and the Financial Accounts of the United States line up well.

To summarize, households appear to report the values of transaction accounts, houses, vehicles (or at least their make and model, from which survey researchers can establish the value), mortgages, auto loans, and perhaps credit card debt fairly accurately. As indicated in Table 3, these well-reported assets comprise about 40 percent of aggregate household assets, whereas these types of debt comprise most aggregate debt.[8] The least-reliable wealth components— retirement accounts, cash value of whole life insurance, and small businesses—represent 33 percent of aggregate assets. Retirement accounts in particular are broadly held, with more than half of households having these accounts. These findings suggest that simply collecting data on categories that are well-reported by households may significantly understate many households' wealth. At the end of this paper, we consider whether information on assets and debt that are well-reported nonetheless can provide reasonable proxies for total worth and changes in wealth.

IV.   Implications for a new panel survey

Options for addressing measurement error

We consider three approaches for addressing measurement error: collect and edit survey data within a framework with more safeguards against measurement error; increase the sample size; or supplement survey data with administrative data that may be measured more accurately.

The first approach draws heavily on the best practices of the SCF and other household wealth surveys such as the new Eurosystem Household Finance and Consumption Survey (HFCS). The SCF emphasizes the prevention of measurement error through careful design and sequencing of the questions; specialized training for the interviewers on household wealth; and ongoing

---

[8] The asset and debt categories shown in Table 3 differ in some instances from those shown in Tables 1 and 2. For example, retirement accounts in Table 3 are the sum of the IRA/Keogh account balances, current-job account-type pensions for the respondent, and past-job pensions shown in Tables 1 and 2 as well as current-job account type pensions for the spouse/partner (if applicable). The calculations for Table 3 were performed in Excel, based on the spreadsheets available at the Federal Reserve website.

monitoring of the survey process for breakdowns.[9] Respondents are encouraged to bring financial records; one way to increase respondents' use of records might be to provide targeted financial incentives for doing so.[10] The SCF survey software incorporates real-time edit checks, conditional routing of questions, and screens that translate numeric dollar amounts into words that are read back to the respondent for confirmation. The SCF invests heavily in data editing that includes review of interviewer comments, as is true as well for surveys that comprise the HFCS (European Central Bank, 2013). The SCF and the HFCS also utilize range and consistency checks.

Some existing longitudinal surveys have experimented with "dependent interviewing," in which respondents are asked during the interview to reconcile their answers with responses given in earlier years. (This approach is conceptually similar to the edit checks in the SCF that ensure that a respondent's answers are consistent *within* each interview.) Several studies based on the British Household Panel Survey indicate that dependent interviewing can improve the accuracy of data on dimensions such as data-entry errors and under-reporting of items such as receipt of income from benefits programs (Jäckle, 2009; Lynn et al., 2012; Lugtig and Jäckle, 2014). This methodology appears to be a promising way to improve data quality, and the introduction of the European HFCS seems likely to spur further research and experimentation in this area in coming years.

A second approach is to increase the sample size of the survey. As noted earlier, the variance of wealth data is high. Increasing the sample size should improve the ability of researchers to estimate statistically significant changes, especially over subgroups. However, in many instances measurement error may be correlated with factors that affect wealth accumulation. Individuals with more financial sophistication, for example, may be wealthier than their counterparts and also more likely to answer surveys accurately. In line with this possibility, Bucks and Pence (2008) show that borrowers with less income are more likely to reply that they "don't know" key terms of their mortgages. It seems likely that a large sample size would

---

[9] Kennickell (2014) provides more information on procedures in the SCF that are designed to reduce measurement error.
[10] Couper, Ofstedal, and Lee (2013) analyze strategies to encourage households to use records in a survey interview. They conclude that these strategies can increase the record use but, at least in the setting they consider, the precision of responses does not improve significantly as a result.

improve the precision of the estimates, but the bias associated with measurement error might persist.

A third approach is to rely more heavily on administrative data. For example, in recent years, researchers have turned to data from credit-bureau files to examine changes in household liabilities. One such example is the Federal Reserve Bank of New York's Consumer Credit Panel, which includes quarterly data from 1999 to the present on household liabilities. (See Lee and van der Klaauw, 2010, and http://www.newyorkfed.org/microeconomics/ccp.html for more information.) These data are substantially more timely than survey data: they are available about a month after the end of each quarter, and reports and analyses of these data are posted regularly on the Federal Reserve Bank of New York's web site.[11] These data have been used, for example, by Lee, Mayer, and Tracy (2013) to explore the role that second mortgage liens played in the mortgage crisis, and by Bhutta (2014) to examine mortgage dynamics during the 1999–2013 mortgage boom and bust. Mian, Rao, and Sufi (2013) have used similar data—albeit aggregated to the zip-code level—to explore the relationship between household debt and spending.

Two major advantages of data from credit bureau files are their size and geographic coverage. The Federal Reserve Bank of New York's data, for example, consist of a five percent random sample of individuals with credit histories; all other individuals living at each sampled person's address are included in the data as well. In total, records corresponding to more than 38 million individuals are included in the data. The data also contain geographic identifiers for each individual down to the census-block level. As a result, the data can be used for precise estimates of changes over time in debt and delinquency, even for narrowly defined groups and geographic regions.

One crucial drawback of credit bureau files is that the data do not include the entire household balance sheet or many characteristics of the household. Credit bureau data provide no information on assets, and some forms of non-traditional credit, such as payday loans, are not reported to the credit bureaus. The data also include very little information on characteristics such as income, employment, or family composition. Researchers often address this limitation by merging census-block demographic characteristics to de-identified data from credit bureaus,

---

[11] See http://www.newyorkfed.org/regional/householdcredit.html

or by inferring family composition from the reported ages of the individuals in the household (see Dettling and Hsu, 2014, for one example). In some cases, researchers have worked with the credit bureaus to match individual-level administrative data from other sources to individual credit records (see Board of Governors, 2007, for one example). Such merges must be consistent with the safeguards in the Fair Credit Reporting Act.[12] In general, though, the missing information on assets and household characteristics implies that credit bureau files are unlikely to be a full substitute for survey data in exploring the dynamics of household wealth accumulation.

Although credit-bureau data are generally considered to be more accurate than survey data, they are not immune from measurement error for a number of reasons. A measure reported in the data, for instance, may not align completely with the relevant concept for research or policy purposes. Some creditors do not report all data fields, some report data with a lag, some do not supply data to all three credit major credit bureaus, and some may supply erroneous data inadvertently.[13] Reporting practices may vary across loan servicers and over time, and when loans are transferred from one servicer to another, they may disappear temporarily from the credit files. Credit bureaus may also lose track of households for a time when households move. Investigations by staff at the Federal Reserve Bank of New York, however, suggest that these data issues may not be empirically important.[14]

A final drawback of credit bureau files is that they are maintained by private companies, and are available to researchers only at fairly high cost. A public-use version of the data would likely limit researchers' interest in purchasing the data directly from the bureaus. As a result, obtaining the rights for a publicly available version could be quite expensive. This expense could limit the financial resources available for other facets of the survey.

Survey data and administrative data are not necessarily separate options. Another possibility is to combine the strengths of both sources of data by linking administrative data to survey records. However, such a linkage would not be a trivial task. Rates of consent to record linkage vary

---

[12] Only de-identified data are provided to researchers.
[13] Brown et al (2014), for example, note in reference to analyzing student loan data with the FRBNY Consumer Credit Panel that "irregularities in student loan reporting prior to 2004 suggest dropping the 1999–2003 data."
[14] Personal communication, Meta Brown, August 12, 2014.

widely across longitudinal surveys, with some studies suggesting a range from as low as about 30 percent to greater than 75 percent (Bricker and Engelhardt, 2013; Korbmacher and Schröder, 2013, and references therein). Given the sensitivity of financial information, it seems likely that the share of respondents that would agree to have their information matched with administrative data would fall in the lower part of this range.[15] Low consent rates are a concern because prior evidence suggests that respondents who agree to record matching are not a representative subsample (Bricker and Engelhardt, 2013; Korbmacher and Schröder, 2013; and Sakshaug et al., 2012).

Developing public-access versions of linked survey and credit bureau data in particular would be challenging. Such a linkage raises the typical concerns about safeguarding respondent privacy, and, as noted above, linking information from credit records would bring the additional complications of complying with the provisions of the Fair Credit Reporting Act. In addition, typically administrative linkages involve government data; in this case, the data are collected by private companies and, as noted above, gaining access to the data could be quite expensive.

Finally, as suggested earlier, debt is relatively well-measured on household surveys. The greater need, from a measurement perspective, is better data on household assets, which credit bureau data cannot address. Perhaps comprehensive administrative panel data on assets will be derived at some point from tax records, property lien data, on-line personal-finance software, or other sources, although some of these data sources may not be representative of U.S. households as a whole.[16] Some such data products exist for nonfinancial assets—Polk collects automobile registration data, for example, and CoreLogic collects property tax and transactions data. However, no analogous products exist for financial assets.

Options for collecting panel wealth data

As noted above, in our assessment, the United States does not currently have a panel survey with sufficiently comprehensive and accurate wealth data to answer some pressing policy questions

---

[15] See Sakshaug et al. (2012) for a discussion of the issues involved in obtaining respondent consent to link administrative and survey records.

[16] Baker (2014), Baugh et al. (2014), and Kuchler (2013) illustrate the usefulness of data from personal-finance websites for research, and Browning et al. (2014) assess the strengths, challenges, and shortcomings of these and other types of administrative data.

related to household wealth and wealth accumulation. Three general strategies for filling this gap come to mind: i) improve the quality of the wealth data on an existing panel survey—most naturally, to our minds, the PSID; ii) add a panel component to the Survey of Consumer Finances; iii) or start a new panel survey. To further the discussion of ways to improve panel wealth data, we provide some thoughts next about the merits of these approaches.

1. Improve the quality of wealth data on an existing panel survey. In considering the possibility of building on an existing panel data, the Panel Study of Income Dynamics appears to be the most promising candidate because it surveys households of all ages.[17] However, we believe that there is scope to improve the accuracy of the wealth data collected in the PSID and, in turn, the usefulness of the data for analyzing policy and research questions.

One possible disadvantage of the PSID is that—like all surveys in the U.S. other than the SCF— it does not oversample households in the top of the wealth distribution. Measuring these households is important for understanding the distribution of wealth as a whole. However, the most pressing policy questions about the adequacy of household saving center on lower- and middle-class households, and standard area-probability samples appear to cover these households adequately. For example, Kennickell (2008) notes that all but the top one percent or so of the wealth distribution appears to be well-captured by the SCF's area-probability sample. Similarly, Bosworth and Anders (2009), Bosworth and Smart (2009), and Pfeffer et al. (2014) document that the distribution of the level of average wealth in the SCF and PSID matches fairly well through at least the 90th percentile. Therefore, we are not particularly troubled by the fact that the PSID does not reflect fully the wealth of high-wealth households.

We are more troubled by the large changes in wealth reported by some households over time in the PSID (Bosworth and Smart, 2009), an issue common to panel wealth surveys (Venti, 2011; Hill, 2006). Some of these large changes seem to stem from inconsistent reports by respondents over time. Increased use of dependent interviewing techniques may be a partial solution. The PSID already asks about some possible reasons for changes in wealth, such as purchase or sale of a property or business, or receipt of an inheritance. Presumably the survey could also ask

---

[17] For the purposes of this discussion, we assume that the PSID data remain representative and have not been compromised over time by attrition or other issues.

whether any of these factors explain any large changes in the levels of wealth from one wave to the next.

We provide some ideas for changes to the wealth questions on the PSID that might reduce respondent burden and improve the accuracy of the data. These recommendations reflect our assessment of best practices in, for example, the SCF and HCFS surveys and received wisdom rather than more rigorous evidence from methodological experiments, cognitive testing, or other research.

- The survey asks for the net values (that is, the value of the asset minus any corresponding debt) for automobiles, stocks, and financial assets. Asking for the asset and debt components separately would likely increase the quality of the data, since many households likely do not think in "net" terms for assets such as vehicles. This change would also provide researchers with richer data on household portfolios. The change would also be a further step in a direction that the PSID has already taken, as the survey appears to have made this change in collecting data on second homes, other types of real estate, and businesses in the 2013 questionnaire.

- The mutual fund questions, which are currently split up on the PSID, could be revised. Stock mutual funds are asked as part of the "do you own stock" question, but bond mutual funds are not mentioned in the 2013 questionnaire. In the 2011 survey, bond mutual funds were asked about jointly with cash value of life insurance, trusts, and valuable collections. This question structure may cause households to under-report mutual funds, especially "balanced" funds that combine stocks and bonds. Tabulations from the 2010 SCF suggest that 17 percent of households that have mutual funds hold a combination stock and bond mutual fund.

- The PSID also groups many types of assets into one question. For example, respondents are asked to report jointly their balances in checking and savings accounts, money market funds, certificates of deposit, government savings bonds, and Treasury bills. Asking separately about some of these assets might prompt respondents to remember more types of assets.

- A comparison of the PSID and SCF (Pfeffer, Schoeni, Kennickell, and Andreski, 2014) suggests that the SCF measures of the values of closely held businesses are much higher than the PSID measures, even when the households in the SCF high-wealth oversample are excluded from the estimates. Businesses are, admittedly, quite hard to value, so perhaps the scope for improving these questions is limited.

- To make room for these new questions, PSID staff might consider streamlining some of the more detailed questions on the pension module. As noted earlier, the existing literature is fairly pessimistic about respondents' ability to answer these questions correctly. The elevated "don't know" rates in the PSID for these questions are consistent with this view. For example, around 45 percent of respondents for whom the question was applicable reported that they didn't know their expected pension benefits upon retirement.

- The "legal bills" question could be dropped, as it does not pertain to many households and is likely not an important factor in wealth dynamics. The cash value of whole life insurance might also be dropped since this asset is poorly measured and is a small component of household wealth.

The survey could also explore supplementing the survey with administrative data for a limited set of variables. For example, the PSID already collects the make, model, and year of the vehicles that the household owns; the survey could generate the vehicle value as estimated by the NADA guides, as is done on the SCF. An external measure of the house value could be generated from Zillow or from local tax assessments, though such information likely could only be released as part of restricted-access of the data. Measures of debt could be generated from credit bureau files, although, as discussed earlier, the privacy and consent issues may prove daunting. Finally, there may be additional avenues for improving data quality by, for example, providing additional interviewer training on financial topics; developing materials for respondents to help them understand, classify, and report various assets and liabilities; and encouraging households to refer to financial records during the interview.

2. Add a permanent panel component to the Survey of Consumer Finances. Given the measurement issues involved in collecting wealth data, a natural approach would be to build on the well-developed SCF infrastructure to collect panel data. This approach would also build on the SCF's research experience when it re-interviewed the 2007 respondents in 2009 in order to capture the full dimensions of the effect of the financial crisis and recession on household balance sheets.

It may not be straightforward to adapt the "SCF model" to a survey intended to address a range of topics. One of the reasons that the SCF data are so high-quality is that the SCF asks detailed questions about almost all components of household wealth. Because the wealth questions are so exhaustive, there is not room on the survey to add extensive batteries of questions on other topics, such as consumption. As it is, the survey takes from around 40 minutes to several hours to complete. The SCF's sample design might further limit the topics that a new longitudinal survey could address: assuming budget constraints are held constant, a consequence of oversampling wealthier households is that fewer households of interest for other topics can be sampled.

In addition, the SCF model has not been tested in the context of long-running panel studies. A primary concern is whether a comprehensive wealth survey like the SCF would be subject to greater nonrandom attrition over time than a survey on another topic. The SCF cross-section obtains a relatively high response rate given the topic and length of the interview, and for the 2007–09 panel, nearly 90 percent of eligible 2007 SCF households participated in a re-interview in 2009. Nonetheless, households may be reluctant to participate in such a lengthy interview on such a sensitive topic numerous times, so attrition could be an even greater concern than for other panel data sources.[18]

As a starting point, one approach to developing longitudinal SCF data would be a sequence of shorter panels. Such panels would be well-suited to analyzing, for example, the immediate effects of policy changes and households' responses to macroeconomic shocks. Other questions, such as the determinants of wealth accumulation and intergenerational wealth mobility, would require data that span a longer period.

---

[18] The experience of the Spanish EFF household wealth survey suggests that refreshment samples can be used to mitigate this concern.

3. *Collecting wealth data as part of a new panel.* Finally, a perhaps obvious question is whether it is possible to collect longitudinal wealth data in a way that borrows from and balances the strengths of the PSID and SCF. We believe that a reasonable starting point would be to forego the SCF's approach of over-sampling wealthier households but incorporate SCF procedures for collecting accurate wealth data such as interviewer training on the particular challenges of collecting financial data, range and consistency checks, and comprehensive editing and imputation.

If resources are limited, one possibility is to collect information on a carefully chosen, abbreviated set of assets and debts with a focus on collecting these as accurately as possible. The aim of such a strategy would be to construct an index that was correlated highly with net worth rather than to estimate net worth itself.[19] This approach would be similar to that of Browning, Crossley, and Weber (2003) and others in measuring household consumption.[20] Such an index might be more useful as a control variable for analyses of other topics than as a dependent variable in a study of wealth accumulation.

In selecting this subset of wealth components, we recommend considering which components appear to be well-reported by households as well as which components help differentiate households by net worth. Prioritizing data on well-reported assets and debts should also reduce the costs of data editing and imputation. As suggested earlier, we recommend collecting data separately by type of accounts—for example, households should be asked separately about checking accounts and savings accounts. However, it is likely sufficient to ask households about all checking account balances in one question, as opposed to querying about each checking account individually.

As an illustrative example of this method and its potential viability, we examine the correlation between total net worth as measured in the SCF and the net value of a limited set of assets and debts in the SCF that our earlier tabulations suggest households report relatively accurately.

---

[19] Evidence from surveys that measure consumption expenditures suggests that asking about a specific subset of expenditures may yield relatively high quality data (see, for example, Winter, 2004, and Browning et al., 2014). In particular, a limited set of questions may strike a favorable balance between under-reporting that appears to occur when respondents are asked a "one-shot" question about total consumption and asking more exhaustive questions that respondents may be less likely to respond to or to respond to accurately.

[20] See Browning et al. (2014) for a review of these approaches.

Specifically, we define a "partial net worth" for both years of the 2007–09 SCF panel that includes the values of checking, savings, and money-market accounts; CDs; mutual funds; stocks; bonds; savings bonds; vehicles; the primary residence and mortgages against the home; education loans; and vehicle loans.[21]

The level of partial net worth is strongly correlated with net worth in the SCF. For both years of the SCF panel, the R^2 for a regression of complete net worth on the partial net worth measure is about 55 percent, and Kendall's tau is about 78 percent.[22] The R^2 increases to nearly 85 percent for a simple regression of a household's percentile rank in the net worth distribution on the household's percentile when ranked by the partial net worth measure. As might be expected, the correlation between changes in net worth and changes in partial net worth is weaker, with a regression R^2 of about 19 percent and Kendall's tau of 55 percent.

These findings suggest that collecting data on a limited set of assets and debts could provide a reasonable proxy for total household wealth. To reap the full benefit of this approach, the limited set of wealth questions on the new panel survey should mirror the wording and ordering of their SCF counterparts to the extent possible. Panel-survey researchers could impute a comprehensive measure of net worth from the full SCF data by using the set of questions that are common to both surveys—including not just assets and debts (as above) but also, for example, age, education and family size.

V.   Conclusions

The U.S. has several panel surveys that collect wealth data. These data have contributed significantly to our understanding of household wealth dynamics. For example, aggregate household net worth declined by 15 percent from 2007 to 2009.[23] However, these wealth declines were not experienced by all households. Bricker et al. (2011), using the SCF data,

---

[21] Equivalently the partial net worth measure excludes the value of: IRA/Keoghs, 401(k)s and other retirement accounts; trusts and annuities; cash-value life insurance; call accounts; businesses; residential and non-residential real estate other than the primary residence and any associated mortgages; credit-card balances; lines of credit (other than home-equity lines of credit); and unclassified assets and debts.

[22] Regressing net worth on all of the individual components included in partial net worth yields an R^2 of about 60 percent.

[23] The decline in aggregate wealth is calculated from the Financial Accounts of the United States. The change is calculated from 2007:Q3 to 2009:Q3, which corresponds roughly with the dates of the SCF survey waves.

indicate that around 60 percent of households lost wealth over this period, but about 25 percent had wealth gains of 27 percent or more.

Despite this abundance of data, our understanding of the long-term determinants of wealth accumulation remains incomplete. All the available datasets have limitations, such as following only specific cohorts of individuals, or spanning short periods of time. More broadly, the considerable measurement issues inherent in wealth data appear to inhibit the ability of researchers, in some cases, to estimate changes in wealth precisely and accurately.

Given the scope of the measurement issues, perhaps researchers should consider alternatives to household-survey panel data to explore wealth accumulation. As described earlier, one possibility is to rely more heavily on administrative data sources, such as credit-bureau records. Another possibility is to combine microeconomic and macroeconomic data. For example, researchers can construct "synthetic" panels from repeated cross-sectional surveys by grouping households by time-invariant characteristics, such as age in a given year, and can disentangle active saving from capital gains by applying aggregate rates of return to household portfolios within each group. Maki and Palumbo (2001) and Sabelhaus and Pence (1999) have used these techniques to explore wealth accumulation patterns during the 1990s. Mian, Rao, and Sufi (2013) follow a conceptually similar approach—using zip-codes as the panel observations—to study the relationship between debt and spending.

These approaches have enriched our understanding of household wealth dynamics, but we believe that household-survey panel data are still an irreplaceable part of the puzzle. Although credit bureau files are a rich source of data on household debt, comprehensive administrative data on household financial assets seems a distant prospect, in part because of the formidable privacy issues involved and the large number of financial institutions with which households invest their money. And synthetic panel techniques, by definition, eliminate much of the identifying variation in the data, a point made by Parker, Souleles, and Carroll (forthcoming) in arguing for maintaining the panel component of the Consumer Expenditure Survey. Moore and Palumbo (2010) provide an illustration of the potential tension between results derived from panel wealth data and those derived from combining macro and micro data. The authors apply the aggregate changes in stock and house prices from 2007 to June 2009 to the portfolios of households in the 2007 SCF. This calculation suggests that only 2 percent of households in the 2007 SCF should have experienced wealth gains of 10 percent or more over the period—whereas Bricker et al (2011), as noted earlier, found that that 25 percent of households in the 2007-09 SCF panel experienced wealth increases of 27 percent or more over this period.

We believe that pairing continued innovation in measurement along with the development of a new household panel survey on wealth—or the refinement of an existing survey—would be an important step towards understanding household wealth accumulation. In considering the next steps, researchers will need to balance the conceptually ideal data to answer the most pressing policy questions, the realities of measurement error, and budget constraints. Researchers may glean some lessons about these tradeoffs from the experiences of the redesigned SIPP, the 2007-09 SCF panel, and the HFCS surveys. We encourage an ongoing dialog between the designers and users of these surveys, survey methodologists, statisticians, and policymakers.

References

Baker, Scott (2014). "Debt and the Consumption Response to Household Income Shocks." Working Paper, Northwestern University.

Baugh, Brian, Itzhak Ben-David, and Hoonsuk Park (2014). "Disentangling Financial Constraints, Precautionary Savings, and Myopia: Household Behavior Surrounding Federal Tax Returns." NBER working paper 19783.

Bhutta, Neil (2014). "The Ins and Outs of Mortgage Debt During the Housing Boom and Bust." Finance and Economics Discussion Series 2014-91 (Washington: Board of Governors of the Federal Reserve System).

Board of Governors of the Federal Reserve System (2007). *Report to the Congress on Credit Scoring and its Effect on the Availability and Affordability of Credit* (Washington: Board of Governors of the Federal Reserve System).

Bosworth, Barry P., and Sarah Anders (2008). "Saving and Wealth Accumulation in the PSID, 1984-2005." Center for Retirement Research at Boston College Working Paper 2008-02.

Bosworth, Barry P., and Rosanna Smart (2009). "Evaluating Micro-Survey Estimates of Wealth and Saving." Center for Retirement Research at Boston College Working Paper 2009-04, http://ideas.repec.org/p/crr/crrwps/wp2009-4.html.

Bradburn, Sudman, and Associates (1979). *Improving Interview Method and Questionnaire Design.* San Francisco: Jossey-Bass.

Bricker, Jesse and Gary V. Engelhardt (2013). "A Test for Selection in Matched Administrative Earnings Data." Finance and Economics Discussion Series 2013-07 (Washington: Board of Governors of the Federal Reserve System).

Bricker, Jesse, Brian Bucks, Arthur B. Kennickell, Traci L. Mach, and Kevin B. Moore (2011). "Surveying the Aftermath of the Storm: Changes in Family Finances from 2007 to 2009." Finance and Economics Discussion Series 2011-17 (Washington: Board of Governors of the Federal Reserve System).

Brown, Meta, Andrew Haughwout, Donghoon Lee, Joelle Scally, Wilbert van der Klaauw (2014). "Measuring Student Debt and Its Performance." Federal Reserve Bank of New York Staff Report No. 668.

Brown, Meta, Andrew Haughwout, Donghoon Lee, and Wilbert van der Klaauw (2013). "Do We Know What We Owe? A Comparison of Borrower- and Lender-Reported Consumer Debt." *Economic Policy Review*, forthcoming.

Brown, Meta, John Karl Scholz, and Ananth Seshadri (2012). "A New Test of Borrowing Constraints for Education." *Review of Economic Studies*, 79:511–38.

Browning, Martin, Thomas F. Crossley, and Guglielmo Weber. (2003). "Asking Consumption Questions in General Purpose Surveys." *The Economic Journal*, 113: F540–F567.

Browning, Martin, Thomas F. Crossley, and Joachim Winter. (2014). "The Measurement of Household Consumption Expenditures." *Annual Review of Economics*, vol. 6, pp. 475–501.

Bucks, Brian, and Karen Pence (2006). "Do Homeowners Know Their House Values and Mortgage Terms?" Finance and Economics Discussion Series 2006-03 (Washington: Board of Governors of the Federal Reserve System), www.federalreserve.gov/pubs/FEDS/2006/200603/200603pap.pdf.

Bucks, Brian, and Karen Pence (2008). "Do Borrowers Know their Mortgage Terms?" *Journal of Urban Economics*, vol. 64, pp. 218-33.

Charles, Kerwin, and Erik Hurst (2003). "The Correlation of Wealth across Generations." *Journal of Political Economy,* 111(6): 1155-82.

Cooper, Daniel (2013). "House Price Fluctuations: The Role of Housing Wealth as Borrowing Collateral." *Review of Economics and Statistics*, 95 (4): 1183–1197.

Couper, Mick P., Mary Beth Ofstedal, and Sunghee Lee (2013). "Encouraging Record Use for Financial Asset Questions in a Web Survey." *Journal of Survey Statistics and Methodology*, 1(2): 171-82.

Dettling, Lisa, and Joanne Hsu (2014). "Returning to the Nest: Debt and Parental Co-residence Among Young Adults." Finance and Economics Discussion Series 2014-80 (Washington: Board of Governors of the Federal Reserve System).

Dynan, Karen E. (2012). "Is a Household Debt Overhang Holding Back Consumption?" *Brookings Papers on Economic Activity*, Spring, pp. 299-344.

European Central Bank (2013). "The Eurosystem Household Finance and Consumption Survey Methodological Report for the First Wave," European Central Bank Statistics Paper Series No 1.

Goodman, John L., and John B. Ittner (1992). "The Accuracy of Home Owners' Estimates of House Value," *Journal of Housing Economics,* 2: 339–57.

Gustman, Alan, Thomas Steinmeier, and Nahid Tabatabai (2007). "Imperfect Knowledge of Pension Plan Type." NBER Working Paper Series 13379.

Henriques, Alice (2013). "Are Homeowners in Denial about their House Values? Comparing Owner Perceptions with Transaction-Based Indexes," Finance and Economics Discussion Series 2013-79 (Washington: Board of Governors of the Federal Reserve System).

Henriques, Alice, and Joanne Hsu (2014). "Analysis of Wealth Using Micro and Macro Data: A Comparison of the Survey of Consumer Finances and Flow of Funds Accounts," in Jorgenson, Dale W., J. S. Landefeld and Paul Schreyer eds., Measuring Economic Sustainability and Progress, Studies in Income and Wealth, Vol 72. Cambridge, MA: National Bureau of Economic Research.

Hill, Daniel H. (2006). "Wealth Dynamics: Reducing Noise in Panel Data." *Journal of Applied Econometrics*, 21: 845-860.

Hurst, Erik, M. C. Louh, and Frank P. Stafford (1998). "Wealth Dynamics of American Families, 1984-1994," *Brookings Papers on Economic Activity*.

Jäckle, Annette (2009). "Dependent Interviewing: A Framework and Application to Current Research." In Methodology of Longitudinal Surveys, edited by Peter Lynn, 93–111. John Wiley & Sons, Ltd.

Juster, F. Thomas, James P Smith, and Frank Stafford (1999). "The Measurement and Structure of Household Wealth." *Labour Economics* 6(2): 253–275.

Kennickell, Arthur (2006). "How Do We Know if We Aren't Looking? An Investigation of Data Quality in the 2004 SCF," http://www.federalreserve.gov/econresdata/scf/files/asa20063.pdf.

Kennickell, Arthur (2008). "The Role of Over-sampling of the Wealthy in the Survey of Consumer Finances." *The IFC's contribution to the 56th ISI Session, Lisbon, August 2007,* vol. 28, Bank for International Settlements, pp. 403-408.

Kennickell, Arthur (2011). "Looking Again: Editing and Imputation of SCF Panel Data." http://www.federalreserve.gov/econresdata/scf/files/ASA2011.1.pdf

Kennickell, Arthur (2014). "Dirty and Unknown: Statistical Editing and Imputation in the Survey of Consumer Finances." Working Paper.

Kiel, Katherine A., and Jeffrey E. Zabel (1999). "The Accuracy of Owner-Provided House Values: The 1978-1991 American Housing Survey," *Real Estate Economics*, 27 (2): 263-98.

Koijen, Ralph, Stijn Van Nieuwerburgh, and Roine Vestman (forthcoming). "Judging the Quality of Survey Data by Comparison with 'Truth' as Measured By Administrative Records: Evidence from Sweden." In Christopher Carroll, Thomas Crossley, John Sabelhaus, (eds.), *Improving the Measurement of Consumer Expenditures*, NBER Book Series Studies in Income and Wealth, University of Chicago Press.

Korbmacher, Julie, and Mathis Schröder (2013). "Consent when Linking Survey Data with Administrative Records: The Role of the Interviewer. " *Survey Research Methods*, 7(2): 115-131.

Kuchler, Theresa (2013). "Sticking To Your Plan: Hyperbolic Discounting and Credit Card Debt Paydown." Working paper, New York University.

Lee, Donghoon, and Wilbert van der Klaauw (2010). "An Introduction to the FRBNY Consumer Credit Panel." Staff Report No. 479, http://newyorkfed.org/research/staff_reports/sr479.pdf

Lee, Donghoon, Christopher Mayer, and Joseph Tracy (2013). "A New Look at Second Liens." In *Housing and the Financial Crisis*, Edward Glaeser and Todd Sinai, eds. Cambridge, MA: National Bureau of Economic Research.

Love, David, Michael Palumbo, and Paul Smith (2009). "The Trajectory of Wealth in Retirement." *Journal of Public Economics*, 93(February): 191-208.

Lugtig, Peter, and Annette Jäckle (2014). "Can I Just Check...? Effects of Edit Check Questions on Measurement Error and Survey Estimates." *Journal of Official Statistics*, 30 (1): 45–62.

Lynn, Peter, Annette Jäckle, Stephen P. Jenkins, and Emanuela Sala (2012). "The Impact of Questioning Method on Measurement Error in Panel Survey Measures of Benefit Receipt: Evidence from a Validation Study." *Journal of the Royal Statistical Society: Series A* (Statistics in Society), 175(1): 289–308.

Maki, Dean M., and Michael G. Palumbo (2001). "Disentangling the Wealth Effect: A Cohort Analysis of Household Saving in the 1990s," Finance and Economics Discussion Series 2001-21 (Washington: Board of Governors of the Federal Reserve System).

Mian, Atif, Kamelesh Rao, and Amir Sufi (2013). "Household Balance Sheets, Consumption, and the Economic Slump," *Quarterly Journal of Economics*, 1687-1726.

OECD (2013). Guidelines for Micro Statistics on Household Wealth. OECD Publishing. http://dx.doi.org/10.1787/9789264194878-en.

Parker, Jonathan, Nicholas Souleles and Chris Carroll (forthcoming). "The Benefits of Panel Data in Consumer Expenditure Surveys" in *Improving the Measurement of Household Consumption Expenditures*, Chris Carroll, Thomas Crossley, and John Sabelhaus eds, University of Chicago Press.

Pfeffer, Fabian T., Robert F. Schoeni, Arthur Kennickell, and Patricia Andreski (2014). "Measuring Wealth and Wealth Inequality: Comparing Two U.S. Surveys." Working paper.

Poterba, James, Steven Venti, and David Wise (2011). "The Composition and Drawdown of Wealth in Retirement." *Journal of Economic Perspectives*, 25 (4): 95-118.

Sabelhaus, John, and Karen Pence (1999). "Household Saving in the '90s: Evidence from Cross-Section Wealth Surveys." *Review of Income and Wealth*, 45(4): 435-453.

Sakshaug, Joseph, Mick P. Couper, Mary Beth Ofstedal, and David Weir (2012). "Linking Survey and Administrative Records: Mechanisms of Consent." *Sociological Methods and Research,* 41: 535-69.

Tourangeau, Roger, Lance J. Rips, and Kenneth Rasinski (2000). *The Psychology of Survey Response*, Cambridge University Press: Cambridge.

Van der Cruijsen, Carin, David-Jan Jansen, and Maarten van Rooij (2014). "The Rose-Colored Glasses of Homeowners," De Nederlandsche Bank Working Paper No. 421, April.

Venti, Steven F. (2011). "Economic Measurement in the Health and Retirement Study," Working Paper, Dartmouth College. http://www.dartmouth.edu/~bventi/Papers/Venti-DMC-review_final_1-22-11.pdf

Venti, Steven F., and David A. Wise (1998). "The Cause of Wealth Dispersion at Retirement: Choice or Chance?" *American Economic Review*, 88(2):185-191.

Winter, Joachim (2004). "Response Bias in Survey-based Measures of Household Consumption." *Economics Bulletin*, 3(9): 1–12

Zagorsky, Jay L. (1999). "Young Baby Boomers' Wealth." *Review of Income and Wealth,* 45(2): 135-156.

Table 1. Reporting rates for ownership of selected assets and liabilities, 2009 wave of 2007–09 SCF

Percent

Type of asset or debt	Original value	Edited value	Don't know	Refused	Missing
Financial assets					
Checking	99.6	0.3	0.0	0.1	0.0
Savings/Money market	99.2	0.7	0.1	0.0	0.0
Certificates of deposit	99.6	0.3	0.1	0.0	0.0
Savings bonds	99.9	0.1	0.0	0.0	0.0
Directly held bonds	99.6	0.2	0.2	0.0	0.0
Directly held stocks	99.3	0.5	0.2	0.0	0.0
Mutual funds	98.8	1.0	0.2	0.0	0.0
IRA or Keogh	96.9	3.0	0.1	0.0	0.0
401(k) or other retirement account (current job)[1,2]	86.6	11.8	0.8	0.0	0.8
401(k) or other retirement account (past job)[1]	89.1	10.4	0.3	0.0	0.2
Cash value life insurance[1]	83.0	16.0	0.7	0.0	0.3
Nonfinancial assets					
Cars, trucks, SUVs, etc.	99.7	0.3	0.0	0.0	0.0
Primary residence[1]	97.3	2.7	0.0	0.0	0.0
Other residential real estate[3]	96.6	3.4	0.0	0.0	0.0
Non-residential real estate[3]	97.1	2.9	0.0	0.0	0.0
Business (actively managed)[1]	98.4	1.6	0.0	0.0	0.0
Business (not actively managed)[1]	98.4	1.6	0.0	0.0	0.0
Liabilities					
Mortgage on home[4]	95.4	4.5	0.0	0.0	0.1
Mortgage on other residential properties[4]	78.6	20.1	0.3	0.0	1.0
Mortgage on non-residential properties[4]	81.0	17.6	0.1	0.1	1.1
Credit card debt	99.5	0.5	0.0	0.0	0.0
Vehicle debt[4]	99.5	0.5	0.0	0.0	0.0
Student loans	99.8	0.2	0.0	0.0	0.0

Source. Authors' calculation based on the 2007-09 Panel Survey of Consumer Finances data, available at http://www.federalreserve.gov/econresdata/scf/scf_2009psurvey.htm

Notes: [1] Ownership and edit code determined from multiple SCF questions; [2] Shares are for employed household heads; [3] Excludes households that reported the only such properties are owned by a business; [4] Shares are for to households that owned the corresponding asset.

Table 2. Reporting rates for values of selected assets and liabilities, 2009 wave of 2007–09 SCF

Percent

Type of asset or debt	Original value	Edited value	Range	Don't know	Refused	Missing
Financial Assets						
Checking	87.3	1.0	9.0	1.3	1.4	0.1
Savings/Money market	84.9	1.0	10.0	1.7	2.3	0.2
Certificates of deposit	84.0	1.2	10.3	1.9	2.6	0.0
Savings bonds	86.6	0.8	10.3	1.6	0.5	0.3
Directly held bonds	75.6	1.0	14.1	4.6	4.4	0.3
Directly held stocks	78.3	0.8	14.7	4.0	1.9	0.3
Mutual funds	79.1	1.8	14.6	2.4	2.1	0.2
IRA or Keogh	78.8	2.3	14.0	2.5	1.8	0.5
401(k) or other retirement account (current job)	68.1	9.4	15.6	5.8	0.6	0.6
401(k) or other retirement account (past job)	69.4	3.7	15.6	9.1	0.0	2.2
Cash value life insurance	59.8	7.1	15.9	15.7	1.2	0.3
Nonfinancial assets						
Cars, trucks, SUVs etc.	87.9	0.7	10.0	1.0	0.0	0.3
Primary residence	85.8	1.6	11.3	0.7	0.0	0.7
Other residential real estate	82.0	5.4	11.1	1.4	0.0	0.1
Non-residential real estate	78.2	3.7	12.7	5.0	0.2	0.3
Business (actively managed)	79.4	2.2	14.0	2.1	0.2	2.2
Business (not actively managed)	66.9	1.3	16.6	12.9	0.1	2.3
Liabilities						
Mortgage on home	83.4	3.8	7.6	0.4	0.4	4.4
Mortgage on other residential	89.3	7.1	3.6	0.0	0.0	0.0
Mortgage on non-residential properties	80.4	7.1	9.6	2.8	0.1	0.0
Credit card debt	93.4	1.1	4.9	0.4	0.2	0.1
Vehicle debt	93.0	0.3	6.0	0.7	0.0	0.1
Student loans	87.2	1.1	10.9	0.9	0.0	0.0

Source. Authors' calculation based on the 2007-09 Panel Survey of Consumer Finances data, available at http://www.federalreserve.gov/econresdata/scf/scf_2009psurvey.htm

Table 3. Ownership rates, value of holdings, and share of total net worth for selected assets and liabilities, 2010 SCF

| Type of asset or debt | Percent with asset or debt | Value conditional on ownership | | Uncond'l mean (thousands) | Share of all assets or debts |
		Median (thousands)	Mean (thousands)		
Financial Assets					
Transaction accounts	92	4	32	30	5
Certificates of deposit	12	20	73	9	1
Savings bonds	12	1	6	1	0
Bonds	2	137	587	10	2
Stocks	15	20	203	31	5
Pooled investment funds	9	80	387	34	6
Retirement accounts	50	44	171	86	15
Cash value life insurance	20	7	28	6	1
Other managed assets	6	70	242	14	2
Other financial assets	8	5	64	5	1
Nonfinancial Assets					
Vehicles	87	15	22	19	3
Primary residence	67	170	261	176	30
Other residential property	14	120	289	42	7
Equity in nonresidential property	8	65	322	25	4
Business equity	13	78	781	103	17
Other	7	15	67	5	1
Liabilities					
Mortgage on primary residence	45	109	152	69	70
HELOC on primary residence	7	26	54	4	4
Other residential debt	5	97	178	10	10
Credit card balances	39	3	7	3	3
Lines of credit not secured	2	6	48	1	1
Student loans	19	13	26	5	5
Vehicle loans	30	10	14	4	4
Other installment loans	12	3	15	2	2
Other	6	5	17	1	1

Source. Tabulations derived from "Historic Tables," internal data, nominal dollars,
http://www.federalreserve.gov/econresdata/scf/files/scf2013_tables_internal_nominal.xls

www.ingramcontent.com/pod-product-compliance
Lightning Source LLC
Chambersburg PA
CBHW080624180526
45168CB00007B/3045